Contents

Introduction

Water play is an accepted feature of preschool and early school education. The ideas in this book will help you to capitalize on the children's enjoyment of water play and to turn their activities into learning experiences.

The activities are designed to lead children into an experimental, questioning and testing attitude towards water. They are based on the six strands of the Qualifications and Curriculum Authority's Desirable Learning Outcomes and, together, will give children a wealth of experiences that will help them to acquire knowledge and understanding in a more meaningful way.

Try to adopt a 'play' approach as much as possible, and be flexible. Whatever the focus of any activity, the children will be learning all kinds of things from it and much will depend on your starting point. Always start from what the children already know, and their interests. You should be able to adapt all the activities in this book to work with either individual children or a small group, without too much problem.

The book uses materials which are likely to be readily available within your class or group's location, or which can be easily gathered or collected from the children's families or carers.

All of the activities are designed to give the children confidence and feelings of achievement which, in turn, will become effective tools for learning.

Activities for 3-5 year olds

Water

 Brilliant Publications

Irene Yates

We hope you enjoy using this book. If you would like further information on other titles published by Brilliant Publications, please write to the address given below.

To avoid the clumsy 'he/she' the child is referred to throughout as 'she'.

Published by Brilliant Publications, The Old School Yard, Leighton Road, Northall, Dunstable, Bedfordshire LU6 2HA

Written by Irene Yates
Illustrated by Kirsty Wilson

Printed in Malta by Interprint Limited

© Irene Yates
ISBN 1 897675 259
The right of Irene Yates to be identified as author of this work has been asserted by her in accordance with the Copyright, Designs and Patents Act 1988.

First published in 1998
10 9 8 7 6 5 4 3 2 1

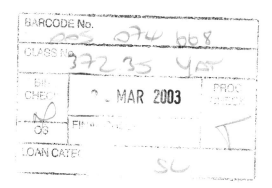

Words, words

What children should learn

Language and literacy – to extend their vocabulary relating to water.

What you need

Water (in water tray or large container), different utensils: eg watering cans (both with and without rose), washing-up liquid bottle, sieve, jug, kettle.

Activity

Play with two or three children at a time, pouring water through different containers from different heights. Show the children how to adjust the speed so that they pour slowly and pour fast. Can they 'catch' the water? Use lots of words to describe what's happening – pour, stream, jet, splash, drip, trickle, plop, splash. Say, for example: 'Let's make a stream of water. Let's make the water trickle.'

Extension

Get the children to listen to the sounds the water makes and to try to describe them.

Talk about

Ask the children if they can make the water drip. Can they make it trickle and splash? What's the difference? How do they make the water behave differently?

Rain words

What children should learn

Language and literacy – to extend vocabulary relating to rain.

What you need

Cards, cotton, felt-tipped pen.

Activity

Ask the children for rain words. Give them some help if they need it. To start them off, you could remind them what it's like on a rainy day. What do they wear to go out? What does the rain feel like? Try to get words like wet, puddle, cloud, raindrop, damp, splish, splash, splosh, soggy.

Extension

Cut three or four large cloud shapes and several raindrop shapes out of card. Write each word on a raindrop. Make a mobile out of the clouds and raindrops, with the raindrops 'falling' from the clouds. Get the children to 'read' the words with you as you hang up the raindrops.

Talk about

Who knows which sound begins the word 'wet' etc. Which sound is at the end of 'splash'? Can you read any of the words to me?

Rainy weather

What children should learn

Language and literacy – to take part in group discussion and improvisation.

What you need

No special equipment.

Activity

Talk about rainy days. Get the children to describe what rain is like, what happens on rainy days. Pretend you're going on a rainy day outing. Lead the children through getting ready to go out. They need to 'put on' their waterproof coats, their wellies, their hats and get an umbrella. Pretend they're outside in the rain, splashing in the puddles. When they 'come in' again, they have to take off the wet clothes and hang them up to dry.

Extension

In pairs, role play two adults meeting at the bus stop in the rain, talking about the weather. Can they find different ways of describing it (eg, raining cats and dogs, pouring, etc)?

Talk about

Why does it rain? Where does rain come from? Why do the children think we need rain? What happens to the rain that falls?

Our water book

What children should learn

Language and literacy – to organize and make a group water book.

What you need

Old catalogues and magazines, scissors, glue stick, sugar paper, wool, felt-tipped pen.

Activity

Work with two or three children at a time but give the whole group the opportunity to participate. Make a book by folding two sheets of sugar paper in half. Tie them together with wool. Ask the children to look through the catalogues and magazines for pictures of water or anything to do with water. Help them sort the pictures into different sets, eg washing machines, kettles, baths, rivers, ponds, rain, etc. Help the children to stick the pictures into the book. Label them with the children's names. Give the book a title: 'Our water book'.

Extension

Keep the book accessible so that the children can look at it alone, together or with another adult at any time.

Talk about

What kind of things might we find in the pictures? What things use water at home? What might have water outside?

Fish in the sea

What children should learn

Mathematics – to recognize numbers and count.

What you need

Two paper plates (painted blue), twelve fish (coloured and cut out), a die with spots, magnet, string, paper-clips.

Activity

This is a game for two children. Make sure they know how to throw the die and help them to count the spots.

The children play 'Fish in the sea' in pairs. Each child has a blue plate (the sea) and six fish. They take it in turns to throw the die. The number it reads is the number of fish that should be in the sea, so they put in (or take out) the appropriate number of fish to make that number. Encourage the children to count out loud each time. The first to have six fish in the sea wins the game. The game starts again.

Extension

Put a paper-clip on the end of each fish. You need a small magnet with a piece of string tied to it. Show the children how to 'catch' the fish in the pond and 'count' them as they catch them.

Talk about

How many fish are in the pond now? Are there too many? Are there enough? How many should we put in? Can you count how many fish? Can you count how many fish there are in and out all together?

Seashell sort

What children should learn

Mathematics – to compare, sort and match seashells.

What you need

Lots of seashells, Plasticine or playdough.

Activity

Start with a discussion about the seashells with the children. Have they ever seen shells before? Have any of them got seashells at home? Show them some of the different types of shells, describing their shapes, textures and sizes. Let the children touch them. Encourage the children, in twos or threes, to sort the shells into different sets. Let them choose for themselves how they are going to categorize the shells – by size, shape, colour, etc.

Extension

Use the sets of shells for counting activities. Get the children to try to make the shapes out of Plasticine or playdough. Encourage them to make the same number, or one more.

Talk about

What do the shells feel like when you run your fingers over them on the inside? Do they feel the same on the outside? How can we describe the different shapes? Can we find any spirals?

Ice cold drinks

What children should learn

Mathematics – to practise counting and one to one correspondence.

What you need

Water, concentrated fruit juice or squash, tumblers, ice cubes, jugs.

Activity

Organize two children at a time to 'help' you make drinks for a small group. With the children, count how many children are in the group and count out the appropriate number of tumblers. Help the children to make up the juice in the jug. Give them turns to pour the juice into the tumblers. Decide how many ice cubes are needed for one per drink, or two per drink, and let the children add them, counting as they do so.

Extension

Use fruit juice or squash to make ice lollies, which the children can eat.

Talk about

If there were one more child, how many drinks and ice cubes would we need? If there were one less child, how many drinks and ice cubes would we need?

Crossing the water

What children should learn

Personal and social development – to work together to problem solve in imaginative play.

What you need

Blue curtaining or blue frieze/sugar paper, different materials (eg, cardboard boxes, small apparatus, pieces of card), pictures of different areas of water (sea, river, lake, etc), construction materials.

Activity

Work with two or three children at a time. Explain to them that there are lots of different expanses of water – sea, lake, pond, river, etc. Show them pictures and tell them what each area of water is called. Tell them how a river goes through land and flows towards the sea.

Make a 'river' with the material or paper. Ask the children to pretend that they are on one side of the river and that they need to devise a way of getting across, by building a bridge or a boat. Have some cardboard boxes to hand, and some bits of card that could be stepping stones, but let them use their own imaginations to decide what to do.

Extension

Let the children make small 'pretend' rivers and use construction materials to build boats or bridges that will cross them.

Talk about

Get the children to explain how they have helped each other to solve the problem. Who did this bit? Who did this? Who had this idea?

Water wheels

What children should learn

Personal and social development – to work together to solve a practical problem.

What you need

A polystyrene plate, a plastic egg box, scissors, a stick, container which is narrow enough for the stick to balance across the top, water.

Activity

Cut the egg box into its small containers. Make a hole through the centre of the plate, big enough for the stick to go through with room for movement. Staple the egg containers around the edge of the plate.

Push the stick through the plate and balance the water wheel on the container. Can the children, taking turns and using water, make the wheel go round?

Extension

Set up the same kind of wheel in the dry sand and wet sand trays and let the children experiment to see if they can get the same results with sand as they did with water.

Talk about

If the water makes this little water wheel go round, what would happen if you had a big wheel? Would it still go round? Would it need more water? Or less? Or the same amount? Would a *huge* water wheel work?

Lots of boats

What children should learn

Personal and social development – to work as part of a group.

What you need

Scissors, plastic egg boxes, Plasticine, stapler, paper, straws, water (in water tray or large container).

Activity

Cut the egg boxes up to make small boats. Put a little bit of Plasticine into the bottom of each boat to stand a straw in. Cut a triangular paper sail for each boat and staple it to the straw. Get the children to sail their boats on the water by blowing them through straws. They will need to be careful not to let the boats crash into each other. Help them to take turns to sail their boats safely.

Extension

Get the children to experiment with other ways of making boats. They could try margarine pots and lids, paper folding, shells, etc. Sing 'Row, row, row your boat'.

Talk about

What makes boats different from things that move on the land? How can you make a boat move? How many different kinds of boats have you seen?

Keeping clean

What children should learn

Personal and social development – to demonstrate that they know how to keep themselves clean.

What you need

Space.

Activity

First, talk about how important it is to keep clean and how water is essential to us for this. Talk through all the ways the children can keep clean and germ free – by washing their hands before eating, after the toilet and activities that get them dirty, by bathing or showering regularly and washing their hair, by brushing their teeth, etc.

Play 'Here we go round the mulberry bush', putting in verses for wash our hands/ wash our faces/ take a shower/ brush our teeth, etc. The children should mime the relevant activities.

Extension

Have the children look after the toys in the home corner by washing them and keeping them clean. Get the children to pretend talk to the toys about how they must look after themselves.

The children could paint themselves with face paints. Make washing the paint off an important part of the activity.

Talk about

What would we do if we didn't have water in our homes? How would we keep clean? Why is water so important to us? Why do we need to wash? What happens if we don't wash?

Bubbles

What children should learn

Personal and social development – to work as part of a group with confidence.

What you need

Bucket, 12 cups of water, 1 cup washing up liquid, 50 ml glycerine (from pharmacy), things to blow bubbles with, eg polystyrene bits with holes poked through, wire coat hangers cut and bent into small pieces, lid rings, funnels, plastic bubble blowers from commercial tubes (optional), paint, paper, straws.

Activity

Have plenty of adult help to organize the making and blowing of bubbles. Let the children pour the cups of water into the bucket, then add the washing up liquid and glycerine. Shake or stir the mixture gently, then take turns dipping in the blowers and blowing bubbles. What happens if they blow hard and fast? What happens if they blow gently? Let the children try catching the bubbles. What happens if they take turns to blow their bubbles? What happens if they all blow at once? Which is best?

Extension

Create bubble blowing pictures by mixing paint to a fairly thick consistency. Add a drop of washing up liquid. Make lots of bubbles by blowing through a straw, yourself, into the paint. Get the children each to lay a paper on top of the bubbles and then let it dry. You can change the pictures slightly by blowing the paint again between each one.

Talk about

Are bubbles light or heavy? What shape are they? Can you blow big ones? Teeny ones? Can you blow a whole string of bubbles? Can you catch a bubble? What happens when you touch one?

Dip and drip

What children should learn

Creative development – to make paint-drip pictures.

What you need

Good quality painting paper, water, mixed paint, straws, sponge, felt-tipped pens or wax crayons.

Activity

Get the children to wet their painting paper with the sponge. Dip a straw into the paint and let it drip onto the wet paper. Let the children decide how many times they want to 'dip and drip'. Can they work out a way of making patterns with their drips? Leave their papers to drip and dry.

Extension

When the papers are properly dry get the children to look at their results and decide what their picture might be. Give them felt-tipped pens or wax crayons to draw in details.

Talk about

What would happen if the paper was dry instead of wet? Would it make any difference? What happens to the paint? What else drips? How can you make something drip?

Rainy day pictures

What children should learn

Creative development – to paint an imaginative picture that expresses an idea of themselves in the rain.

What you need

Painting easels, paper, paints, brushes, water pots, protective clothing.

Activity

Get the children to paint pictures of themselves and their friends in the rain. They might show themselves splashing in puddles or huddling under umbrellas. When the painting is finished, get them to dip their brush into the water pot and 'splatter' the picture to make the rain.

Extension

Cut out little umbrellas and stick them to the pictures in the appropriate places.

Talk about

What happens when it rains? What do we wear in the rain? How can we keep ourselves dry?

Water sounds

What children should learn

Creative development – to respond to watery words with percussion instruments.

What you need

Space, percussion instruments such as tambour, drum, hand bells, or home-made items such as rice in washing up bottles, etc.

Activity

You need one instrument per child. Have a collection of watery sound words ready in your head. For example: trickle, drip, rush, gush, plop, splash, splosh, glug. Get the children to try to describe the sounds and then to make appropriate noises with the percussion instruments.

Extension

Create a short repetitive piece. It might be trickle/ trickle/drip/drip/drip/splash/splosh in words. Get the children to 'play' it with percussion instruments.

Talk about

Ask how does a 'trickle' sound – is it a quiet, slow, wobbly sound or a quick, sharp, loud sound? What about splashing, or glugging, etc?

Make a frog

What children should learn

Creative development – to make frog puppets and use the puppets for imaginative play.

What you need

An old small sock for each child (ask parents/carers to send in), small round sticky labels, black felt-tipped pen.

Activity

Make a puppet for yourself first to demonstrate to the children. Take two round sticky labels and draw a black circle on each. Fill the circle in with black. Put the sock on your hand. Stick the eyes on the frog in the appropriate place. Let your frog talk to the children. Help the children to make their own frogs in the same way. Encourage the children to make their frogs talk to each other. For example, one children could pretend that her frog lives in a lovely, deep pond. She could get her frog to invite the other frogs for a special deep water swimming party.

Extension

Teach the children the song: 'Five little speckled frogs sat on a speckled log, eating the most delicious flies. One jumped into the pool, where it was nice and cool, then there were four speckled frogs', etc.

Talk about

Where do frogs live? How do frogs get to be frogs? What are baby frogs called? How are they different?

Off for a swim

What children should learn

Creative development – to create an imaginative movement sequence in response to a story.

What you need

Space, tambour, pictures of pond, ducks, ducklings.

Activity

Show the children the pictures of ducks and ducklings. Talk about how ducklings hatch from eggs and how the mother duck looks after the ducklings, keeping them warm and dry. When the ducklings are only a few days old the mother duck waddles the ducklings off to the pond to teach them to swim. The ducklings follow in a line behind her. Have the children practise waddling like a duck.

Divide the children into groups of four or five, one child being the mother duck, the others being the ducklings. First the ducklings curl up tight, then hatch out of their eggs. The mother duck sits beside them, feeding them and looking after them, then she tells them it's time for them to go for a swim.

Play the tambour in a slow rhythm for the ducklings to follow the mother duck down to the pond, then they all jump in with a splash and make gliding movements to show how they swim around. Go through the sequence again, changing the mother duck so that the children take turns to lead.

Extension

Tell the children how the ducks do 'uptails' to catch food under the water. Can the children work out a way of doing this for themselves?

Talk about

How can we waddle like ducks? Which bits of our body could be our wings? What are ducks' feet like? How do you think ducks swim?

Water movements

What children should learn

Physical development – to move with increasing body awareness and control.

What you need

Space, a running tap.

Activity

First, in pairs, let the children hear and see the running tap, noticing how the water trickles, rushes, gushes and drips. Let them watch as the water spins and swirls as it goes down the plug hole (this could be done as part of a washing up activity, to avoid wasting water).

With the whole group, get the children to recreate the movements of the water with their bodies, eg tiptoeing for the trickling; strong, splashy movements for gushing; staccato movements for dripping; spinning for going down the plug hole.

Extension

With the children, create a movement sequence that they can repeat.

Talk about

Which is the loudest sound, a trickle or a drip? Which is the strongest movement, a gush or a trickle? Which way does the water spin and swirl? How can you change your movements to make them stronger or lighter?

Melting ice

What children should learn

Physical development – to show with body movements how water freezes into ice and thaws again.

What you need

Lots of space.

Activity

Work with the whole group and join in with the role play yourself. Talk about cold and frosty weather and describe to the children what icicles are in case they have never seen them. Describe Jack Frost and how he might have icicles for fingers and toes. Each child pretends to be an icicle – making short staccato movements with jagged fingers and elbows and knees, etc. Try to get a spiky quality to the movements. Get the children to stretch in long, thin shapes. Call for them to 'freeze' several times.

Extension

Get the 'icicles' to melt very, very slowly, each part of the body thawing in turn so that the children melt slowly and curl and droop until they end in a small fluid shape on the floor. Make icicles in the freezer compartment of a fridge and watch them melt.

Talk about

What is ice like? Is it soft and curly or sharp, spiky and jagged? Can you make your whole body spiky – your hands, your fingers, your face, even your eyes and teeth? How does ice melt – what is it like now?

Frogs in the pond

What children should learn

Physical development – to move confidently and imaginatively, to handle objects safely.

What you need

Space, bean bags, a large piece of paper or cloth (eg an old sheet), adhesive tape.

Activity

Tape a large piece of paper or cloth to a space on the floor. It is the pond, and the children are the frogs. Start with all the frogs in the pond. Show them how to do frog jumps, using both hands and feet. When you call 'Frogs out' they all jump out of the pond. The bean bags are flies. Throw a fly to each frog. If they catch it they can jump back into the pond. Get the frogs in the pond to throw the flies back to you and start again.

Extension

Get the children to balance the flies on different parts of their bodies – their heads, their backs, their shoulders, their arms. Can they frog jump with a fly on their head?

Talk about

Frogs can live on land and in the water. What else might be in the pond besides the frogs? What else do they know that lives in the water?

Bubble dance

What children should learn

Physical development – to move freely and lightly like a bubble.

What you need

Lots of space, tambour or drum.

Activity

You can do this with the whole group. First make sure they know how bubbles behave when you blow them and when they burst (see *Bubbles*, page 15) .

Get the children to spread out in a big circle as though they're a huge soap puddle on the floor. Use a tambour or a drum to get the children to turn themselves into big puffed-up bubbles, moving slowly to your beat. Encourage them to whirl and twirl. Tiptoe amongst the children touching them. Burst bubbles fall gently to the ground after one high jump into the air.

Extension

Get the children to talk in front of the group, describing how it might feel to be a bubble floating in the air, and where they might float to.

Talk about

Who has bubbles in the bath? Can they each blow bubbles through the bubble wand? Use words like float, drift, gentle, burst, explode.

Water play

What children should learn

Knowledge and understanding of the world – to explore the properties of water.

What you need

Water (in water tray or large container), bowls, jugs, pots, plastic bottles, yoghurt pots, beakers, plastic cups, etc.

Activity

Let the children play in pairs. Can they find pots or plastic cups that float? How much water do they think could go into the pots before they sink? What happens if you make holes in the pots, in different places in each one? Can they make a transparent bottle half-full of water? Can they make a full bottle half-empty?

Extension

Use different sized and shaped containers. Put one cupful of water into each container. Look at the water levels. Do the children think there is the same amount of water in each, or more, or less?

Talk about

Can you pour all the water from a little container into a big one? Can you put all the water from a big container into a little one? Can you make something that floats, sink? What do your hands look like under the water?

Moving water

What children should learn

Knowledge and understanding of the world – to explore how water moves.

What you need

Water (in water tray or large container), kitchen implements (such as wooden spoon, spatula, slice, hand whisk, slotted spoon, sieve), small container, bucket.

Activity

Work in pairs. Encourage the children to use the implements to try to push the water to and fro in the bowl. Which implements have the best pushing action? Experiment with different materials and implements. Try to find paddle-shaped things which have a strong pushing action.

Extension

Put water into a small container and try using the implements again. Is it easier to move the water about when there is less of it? Which is the best implement to use to fill a bucket? Can they fill a bucket using a slotted spoon?

Talk about

What happens when the water moves? Where does it go? What happens when you use something with holes in it? Would it be better to swim with your fingers spread open or closed? Why?

Freeze, freeze

What children should learn

Knowledge and understanding of the world – to explore how water freezes and thaws.

What you need

Several balloons of different shapes and sizes, water, a freezer compartment, trays, large container of water, food colouring, salt.

Activity

Let the children fill the balloons with water, then freeze them overnight. Next day get the balloons out and pop them to free the frozen water. Put them on trays. Encourage children to touch and handle the frozen shapes. Get them to describe what they can see. Put the shapes into a container of water and watch them melt.

Extension

Let the children drop food colouring on the ice blocks. It soaks in, down the cracks and makes great patterns. You could also investigate sprinkling salt on the ice blocks.

Talk about

What happens when water gets very, very cold? What does it look like? What does it feel like? How has it changed? What do we call water when it's frozen? What will happen to the ice when we float it on the water?

Floating and sinking

What children should learn

Knowledge and understanding of the world – to observe that some things float and others sink.

What you need

Water (in water tray or large container), items such as corks, pebbles, pieces of wood (matchbox or similar), coin, spoon, bottle tops, sponge, pumice stone, soap, fabric, seashells.

Activity

Show the children how a cork floats and a pebble sinks. Line up all the objects and get the children to guess which ones will sink and which ones will float. Let the children take turns putting the objects into the water and seeing if their predictions are right.

Extension

Make a poster showing the two groups. Let the children draw pictures and cut them out, then stick them in the appropriate column.

Talk about

Get the children to predict which things they think will float and which things they think will sink. Does it make any difference how large or small something is, or how heavy it weighs?

Getting things wet

What children should learn

Knowledge and understanding of the world – how different materials absorb or do not absorb water.

What you need

Flannels, different types of sponges (natural, synthetic, large, small), water (in water tray or large container), small containers, a piece of wood, Plasticine, polystyrene, a chamois leather.

Activity

Work with two or three children. Give the children the flannels and the different types of sponges in the water tray. Get them to play with the flannels and sponges, seeing how much water they soak up, how heavy they get and how much water the children can squeeze out. Can they fill a container by squeezing out a sponge into it?

Extension

Give the children other objects such as a piece of wood, Plasticine, polystyrene or a chamois leather, to see whether they will soak up any water.

Talk about

Get the children to describe what's happening. Give them lots of water words – wet, dry, soak, slippery, squeeze, wring, absorb.

Grow cress

What children should learn

Knowledge and understanding of the world – to see how things grow and change.

What you need

A packet of cress seeds, polystyrene tray, paper towels, water.

Activity

Wash the polystyrene tray to make sure it's clean. Spread a double thickness of paper towels in it. Pour some water on the paper towel to make it damp. Sprinkle the cress seeds on the top. Put the tray on a sunny windowsill and look at it everyday. If the paper towel is dry, add some water. The seeds must be kept damp to stop them shrivelling up. Watch the seedlings grow.

Extension

When the seedlings look ready, about 25 cm tall, cut them off and make sandwiches for the children to try.

Talk about

Does the cress need water? How can you tell? What does the water do? How big are the plants now? Are they all growing exactly the same amount each day?

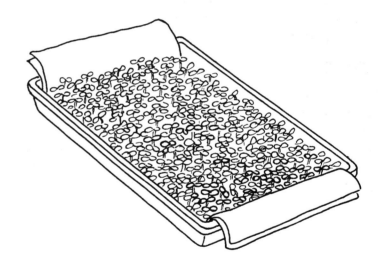

Raisins can dance

What children should learn

Knowledge and understanding of the world – to observe what happens when water, vinegar, bicarbonate of soda and raisins are mixed together.

What you need

Large transparent container, pint of water, several teaspoons of vinegar, tablespoon of bicarbonate of soda, raisins, a long handled spoon, paper, crayons, black tissue paper, glue.

Activity

Work with a small group of children. Let them help you to put the ingredients together. First, put the water into the container. Pour in several spoonfuls of vinegar and stir the mixture. Drop the raisins into the liquid. Now add the spoonful of bicarbonate of soda, but don't be tempted to stir. Watch what happens! When the raisins stop dancing, give the container a little shake.

Extension

Draw pictures of the raisins dancing. Cut 'glass' shapes out of paper, one for each child. Give them black tissue paper to scrunch up and stick on as their dancing raisins.

Talk about

Talk about how the raisins 'rise to the surface'; or 'float to the top' and how they 'sink back down again'. What happens to the raisins before they sink?